Do Bugs Have Noses?

Debby Anderson

CVP

Chariot Victor Publishing
A Division of Cook Communications

Acknowledgements:

Elisa Anderson, my twelve-year-old research assistant on the gooey-ducks of the Pacific Northwest.

To Dr. Ray Bohlin, Ph.D. in molecular and cell biology is executive director of Probe Ministries; and to Sue Bohlin, Probe speaker and women's Bible teacher.

Probe's mission is to communicate the Christian worldview in areas such as the sciences, art, and history. If you are interested in their radio program, *Mind Games* conference, literature, or college forums, please call: 1-800-899-7762, or visit their website at www.probe.org

Barry Wheeler, for our family portrait.

troodon

Chariot Victor Publishing,
a division of Cook Communications, Colorado Springs, Colorado 80918
Cook Communications, Paris, Ontario
Kingsway Communications, Eastbourne, England

DO BUGS HAVE NOSES?
© 1999 by Debby Anderson for text and illustrations

Designer: Nancy L. Haskins
Edited by Jeannie Harmon

First printing, 1999
Printed in Singapore
01 00 99 98 97   5 4 3 2 1

Library of Congress Cataloging-in-Publication Data

Anderson, Debby.
    Do bugs have noses?/Debby Anderson.
        p. cm.
    Summary: Examines God's animal world, emphasizing the role of
creativity in creation and discussing how and why God created animals. Each
chapter includes a Bible Time study, a question to answer, a Scripture, and a
prayer.
    ISBN 0-7814-3060-7
    1. Animals--Religious aspects--Christianity Juvenile literature.
2. Creation Juvenile literature. [1. Animals--Religious aspects--Christianity.
2. Creation. 3. Christian life.] I. Title.
BT746.A53   1999   99-23958
231.7'65--dc21   CIP

15.99

pelican

CONTENTS

manatees

Dear family and friends,

"Do only bees make honey? Do worms live in the mud? Do rocks ever die? Do bugs have noses?" All these delightful questions were launched my direction while my son and I sat together on the front porch. And so began *Do Bugs Have Noses?*

Designed as a resource for the zillions of questions a child asks, *Do Bugs Have Noses?* also provides a *Bible Time* study at the end of every chapter. Each *Bible Time* includes a question to answer, a Scripture, and a prayer. Enjoy reading this book together with your child at bedtime or while you sit together on your front porch!

Debby Anderson

For my son, Kevin, age 7, whose love
for His Creator and curiosity about
His creatures energized this book.

And for family pets everywhere,
especially our faithful pet toads,
Luke and Leia Skyhopper

Creek! **Creek!**

Squoosh!

"In the beginning God
created the heavens and the earth."

Genesis 1:1 NIV

"Then God said,
'Let the earth be filled with animals.'"

Genesis 1:24 NCV
(the Bible's first book!)

Bzzzzz!

Hoo!

Tweet!

Chirp!

Oink!

Cluck!

Ee-ee!

Cheep, cheep,
cheep!

Rumble!

Welcome to the wonderful world of animals!

From stomping, stampeding buffaloes to fluffy, feathery flamingoes,

God's incredible world is filled with animals that

glide and slide

flying squirrel

harp seal

and chase and race.

dog

cat

mouse

buffalo

Our all-powerful God used His all-knowing mind to create an amazing collection of creatures—some dressed in fur or feathers,

shells or quills,

some plain, striped, or polka-dotted!

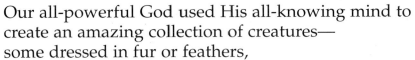

crab

tiger

cougar

porcupine

snow leopard

Every tiger wears different stripes, but behind each tiger's ear is the same white and black circle.

Buffalo used to roam in large herds and gave the Native Americans food, moccasins, clothes, blankets, bags, packs, cooking pots, ropes, quivers, bowstrings, saddles, shields, glue, spoons, tools, and tepees.

With hundreds of different animals to look at, hundreds of different questions come into our minds:

What's inside a prairie dog hole?

Do crocodiles go to the dentist?

snowy owl

Arctic hare

husky

While wallowing in their winter wonderland,
can wide walruses whistle with wet whiskers?

Whoa! Who knows? God knows! He made them.
Together, let's ask questions and try to discover the answers.

BIBLE TIME

- What favorite animal do you want to ask about?
- *"But ask the animals, and they will teach you, or ask the birds of the air, and they will tell you. Speak to the earth, and it will teach you, or let the fish of the sea tell you. Every one of these knows that the hand of the Lord has done this. . . . only God has wisdom and power. . . ." (Job 12:7-13 NCV)*
- Dear God, thank You for making all the animals!

Why is it important to know about the animals?

 Studying the animals helps us to know about God! *"There are things about God that people cannot see—his eternal power and all the things that make him God. But since the beginning of the world these things have been easy to understand by what God has made. . . ."* (Romans 1:20 NCV). The more we know about the animals, the more we know about the God who made them!

Turtles remind us that God is slow to get angry!

Puppies and kittens remind us that God is kind!

The majestic lion reminds us that God is the King of kings!

"A lion, mighty among beasts, who retreats before nothing." (Proverbs 30:30 NIV)

The birds remind us that God is Truth. God made the birds to protect their chicks with their wings. In the same way, God protects us with His truth.

"He will cover you with his feathers, and under his wings you can hide. His truth will be your shield and protection."
(Psalm. 91:4 NCV)

Does God have feathers? No! But just like feathers protect baby birds, God's truth protects us from evil. You can find God's truth in the Bible.

In the Bible, God asks us:
"Does the hawk take flight by your wisdom and spread his wings toward the south?"
(Job 39:26 NIV)

"Do you give the horse his strength or clothe his neck with a flowing mane?"
(Job 39:19 NIV)

Only God is wise and powerful enough to do these things.

"Rock badgers are not very powerful, but they can live among the rocks."
(Proverbs 30:26 NCV)

12

worm

mosquito

So why did God make squirmy worms and biting bugs and slithering slugs? Ugh! In nature, everything has its place. Bugs are breakfast and slugs are supper for many creatures. Worms tunnel and help the soil.

Remember when Adam and Eve sinned in the garden and disobeyed God's rules? Everything changed for the WORSE . . . stings and bites, and sickness, and our pets can die. Animals eat each other and are frightened of people. But sometime soon God will change everything for the BETTER! Jesus says, "Yes, I am coming soon.' Amen. Come, Lord Jesus." (Revelation 22:20 NIV)

ant

slug

scorpion

chimpanzee

Golden monkey

Rhesus

marmoset

BIBLE TIME
• Why do you think God made monkeys and apes? (Maybe just for fun!)
• "Come to me . . . and let me teach you, for I am gentle and humble . . ." (Matthew 11:28-30 TLB)
• Lord, please teach me all about You and Your animals.

Orangutan

Where did the animals come from?

The animals came from God! God is smarter and more powerful than anyone. He spoke the words and it happened! The Bible tells us that *"long ago by God's word the heavens existed and the earth was formed (2 Peter 3:5 NIV); "In the beginning was the Word . . . through him all things were made. . . . In him was life. . . . " (John 1:1, 3, 4 NIV); "By faith we understand that the universe was formed at God's command" (Hebrews 11:3 NIV); "For by him all things were created: things in heaven and on earth, visible and invisible . . . in Him all things hold together" (Colossians. 1:16, 17 NIV).*

In the beginning, God created the heavens and the earth.

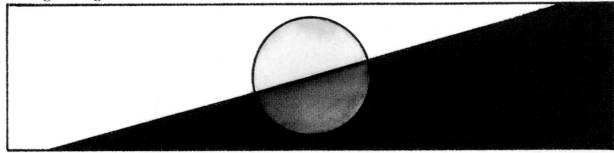

The first day: light!

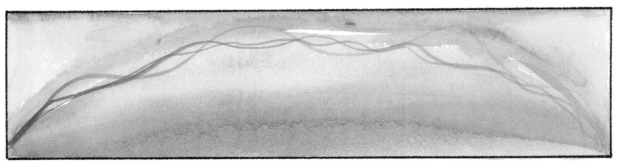

The second day: sky

The third day: land, seas, and plants.

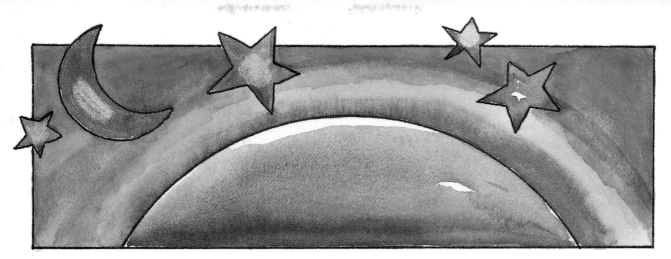

The fourth day: sun, moon, and stars.

The fifth day:
birds and water animals.

The sixth day: land animals
(wild, tame, and ground-crawlers)
and then PEOPLE!

God keeps much of how He created the earth a secret because He wants us to enjoy the adventure of exploring it. Maybe you will grow up to be a scientist and discover new clues, new fossils, maybe even a six-foot dinosaur tooth!

Did this dino brush his teeth every night? Who knows? God knows.

But some scientists don't know God yet. A few people think we began as watery ooze that changed into frogs, then rats, then ape-like animals, then people. But the Bible says, *"God created man in his own image . . ."* (Genesis 1:27 NIV). Maybe you will grow up to be a scientist and help other scientists know about God's love for them.

Animals do change within the limits God carefully designed for them, but they do not magically mutate over millions of years!

There are no furry fish or feathery fox fossils to show changes from critters in ooze . . . to kids in shoes!

ring-tail possum

echidna

Still, we certainly see some strange sights, especially in Australia!

BIBLE TIME
• Which day of creation would you like to watch?
• *"In the beginning God created the heavens and the earth."* (Genesis 1:1 NIV)
• Our Creator, we praise You because You are wiser and more powerful than anyone.

The platypus and echidna are the only two animals with fur that lay eggs.

platypus

How do giraffes sleep?

Giraffes skillfully sleep leaning against trees! God designed animals with different skills, looks, and movements. This is another way we know that God made the animals. Their incredible, amazingly fantastic, delightful DESIGN shouts it out to us! Animals are God's artwork!

From their toes . . .

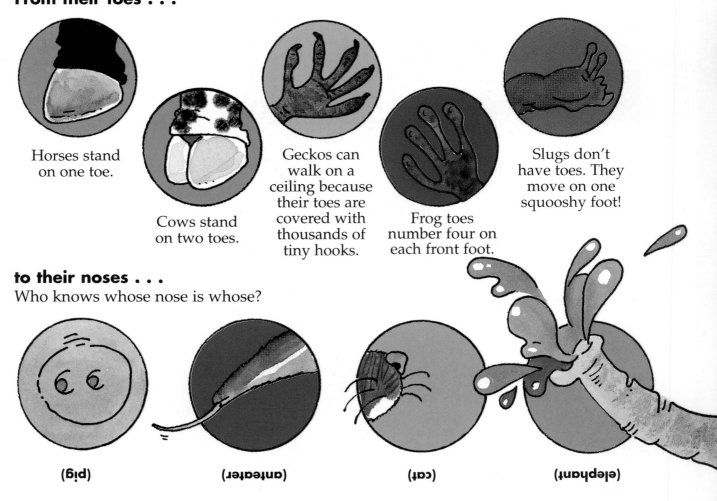

Horses stand on one toe.

Cows stand on two toes.

Geckos can walk on a ceiling because their toes are covered with thousands of tiny hooks.

Frog toes number four on each front foot.

Slugs don't have toes. They move on one squooshy foot!

to their noses . . .

Who knows whose nose is whose?

(pig)

(anteater)

(cat)

(elephant)

God designed each animal with a different **look!**

Texas Longhorns' horns stretch as far as your mattress!
Horny toads sleep buried in sand!

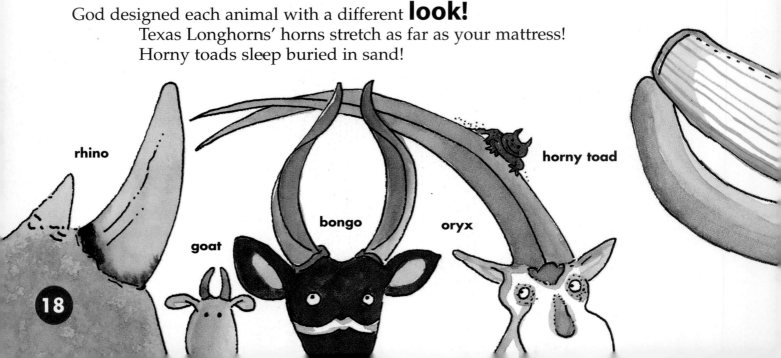

rhino

goat

bongo

oryx

horny toad

parakeet

slow sloth

giraffe

God designed each animal with different **skills!**
Some parakeets sleep hanging upside down!
Bird feet stay locked on the branch even while they sleep.

The slow sloth sleeps and eats hanging sideways.

And God designed each animal with different **movements!**

"*. . . I don't understand: the way an eagle flies in the sky, the way a snake slides over a rock. . . .*" (Proverbs 30:18-19 NCV)

Texas longhorn

Butterflies flutter by.

Cats climb.

BIBLE TIME
- What is your favorite way to move? (Skipping, swimming, running, etc.)
- *"For in Him, we live and move and have our being."* (Acts 17:28 NIV)
- Dear Lord, only You could design so many different looks, skills, and movements!

Frogs flip-flop and float.

Platypuses plop.

Pigs wiggle and wallow.

Ducks wade and waddle.

Fish swish.

Catfish cruise.

Lizards lounge.

Termites tunnel in tall towers.

Aardvarks park in the dark and tangle tangy termites on their ticklish tongues.

21

Are we animals?

Some people think we are animals. They think people have no choice between good and bad. Some people think we are gods and that good and bad are the same. But, yippee! The Bible says we are not animals, we are not gods, we are people—no more, no less.

We are different from the animals because we are God's grand finale . . . like the frosting on the cake, the winning touchdown, the cherry on the sundae! *"Then God said, 'Let the earth be filled with animals'. . . God saw that this was good. Then God said, 'Let us make human beings in our image'. . . God looked at everything he had made, and it was VERY good. . . ."* (Genesis 1:24-31 NCV)

After God made the flyers, the creepy crawlers, and the swimmers, He saw that His creation was good. But after He added people, He saw that all of His creation was VERY good!

Chow time!

A dinosaur driving a dump truck full of dino dinner deluxe!

We are also different from the animals because God took extra care in designing us. *"I praise you [Lord] because you made me in an amazing and wonderful way. . . . "* *(Psalm 139:14 NCV).* Our bodies are similar in design to the animals, but we are more than just bodies. We are human beings! We think, talk, write, laugh, and feel in millions of ways that animals can not.

When was the last time you saw:

Cheetahs cheating at checkers.

A tiger talking tenderly in Thailand.

A kangaroo cooking cupcakes in her country kitchen.

A cow creatively composing on a keyboard? (But cows do give more milk when the farmer plays music!)

An elephant examining extra X-rays.

23

We show love to our parents by obeying them.

Clean your room!

Play with the baby.

Telephone Grandma and Grandpa.

Listen.

Help Mom wash the dishes.

Take care of your pets, because one of God's first commands was to protect the animals.

Smile!

Help a neighbor pull weeds.

24

But the biggest reason we are different from the animals is because . . .
GOD MADE US IN HIS OWN IMAGE! We are His shining lights . . . His
reflections . . . His very own image! We reflect God's image by being like
Him. To be like Him is to show love to others!

Share your tree
and tell a friend
about Jesus.

Write a homesick
missionary a letter.

Hug your Dad.

BIBLE TIME
• What can you do to shine and show God's love to others?
• *"Be imitators of God . . . and live a life of love"* (Ephesians 5:1, 2 NIV); *"For we are
God's workmanship, created in Christ Jesus to do good works"* (Ephesians 2:10 NIV)
• God, please remind me to show Your love to others. Thanks.

Are we animal helpers?

Yes! We are also different from the animals because God gave us the job of protecting and caring for the animals.

toucan

otters

dolphin

panda

lioness and cubs

In the beginning, one of the very first things God told Adam and Eve to do was to *". . . Rule over the fish in the sea and the birds of the air and over every living thing that moves on the ground." (Genesis 1:28 NIV).* Imagine what living in the Garden of Eden must have been like!

God even gave Adam the fun job of naming each animal!
Can you name some of these?

monkey

gazelle

cheetah

dragonfly

goldfish

cooter

gorilla

ladybug

butterflies

But Adam and Eve chose to sin and disobey God's rules, just as each of us has chosen to sin. Because of these choices, the world is all messed up. The animals need our help now more than ever. Room to run, to find food, and to raise a family is disappearing . . . so is clean air and water. But we can help!

REUSE Try to use everything more than once. Grocery bags can be filled again and again. Then fewer trees are cut down to make more bags, and the birds and squirrels can rest in their nests.

REDUCE The fewer things we use, the fewer things are taken from the animals. Turn the water off while you brush your teeth. When we use less water, then more water stays in the lakes and rivers.

RECYCLE Two-liter soda bottles can be recycled into flakes, then melted and spun into fibers. A fleecy jacket can be knitted from the fibers of twenty bottles!

Learn about the animals.

Take care of the animals who live near you . . . especially your pets. Remember, God created them too.

Keep the places around you clean.

Maybe you can even grow up to be a scientist or a veterinarian or a ranger!

raccoon

rabbit

woodchuck

porcupine

weasel

But right now, you can explore and discover!

oriole

screech owl

blue jay

chipmunk

black bear

squirrel

toads

beaver

box turtle

fox

In the beginning, God commanded Adam and Eve to care for the animals. Later, God told Noah to protect the animals by building an ark. Now, it's our turn!

Did Noah and his family chase, capture, and catch that crowd of critters? No, the animals just came! God did a miracle and, when the ark was full, God safely slammed the door shut.

When the rains had come and gone, God told Noah it was time to head 'em out. This was the noisiest, happiest parade anybody had ever seen. Yippee-i-ay!

BIBLE TIME
- What is something you can reduce, reuse, or recycle?
- "I see the moon and stars, which you created . . . But why are people important to you? . . . You put them in charge of everything you made. . . . Lord, our Lord, your name is the most wonderful name in all the earth!" (Psalm 8:3, 4, 6, 9 NIV)
- Lord, remind me to take good care of our animals, just as Noah did.

Hurry!

Are animals people helpers?

Look and see!

When parts of our bodies don't work well, a trained animal can help.

Labrador retriever

Animals warm us with woolly clothes.

sheep

camel

Animals give us food . . . even fresh, foamy milk.

goat

Animals carry us and our stuff where we want to go!

silkworm moth

honeybee

Bugs, bees, butterflies, and all sorts of insects are among the most helpful animals of all! Only a few kinds of insects are troublemakers. The rest feed the songbirds, pollinate the plants, eat the plant-eater bugs, and make wax, silk, and honey.

ladybugs

macaque

bullfrogs

Animals help us to play
. . . hippity hop over the top!

Animals help us to work! . . .
Plippity plop, watch it drop!
Malaysian macaque monkeys
can pick 500 coconuts a day!

33

To make seeds, flowers need to share their pollen with each other. But they can't carry the pollen to the flower next door or mail it in an envelope! Bees help the flowers by carrying the pollen from flower to flower.

Bouncing back and forth, the bee's furry legs become covered with sticky pollen. At each stop, some of the pollen drops off and more sticks on!

The bee also sucks out the flower's sweet nectar and carries it back to the hive. The bees change the nectar into honey by taking water out of it.

Imagine a world without these pollen carriers. There would be only a few oranges or flowers . . . and NO apples, grapes, cotton, or clover!

Imagine a world without God's Word, the Bible. There would be no truth, no rules to keep us safe, no stories of God's love and care, no promises of our home in heaven.

"God's laws are perfect. They protect us, make us wise, and give us joy and light. God's laws are pure, eternal, just. They are more desirable than gold. They are sweeter than honey dripping from a honeycomb." (Psalm 19:7-10 TLB)

What are some of God's laws? Be kind, pray about everything, show respect, be thankful, obey your parents. . . . Do you know any more?

Sweeter than honey, richer than gold . . . let's read and obey God's Word every day! Buzzzzzzzzzzzzzz

BIBLE TIME
- Tell me one of God's laws that you want to obey tomorrow.
- *"How can a young person live a pure life? By obeying your word." (Psalm 119:9 NCV)*
- God, thank You for sweet honey and for the Bible!

How can we learn who the animals are?

One of the best ways to learn about animals is to list them in groups. Let's group them by size. OOPS! What a super blooper! Moose is squooshing rhino's toes!

Many of the biggest animals, like the elephant, giraffe, gorilla, and rhino, eat only veggies! Three cheers for salad. Hip, hip, hooray! The oxpecker bird eats the bugs that eat the rhino!

The gorilla is the biggest ape.

The python is the biggest snake.

The moose is the biggest deer.

The Kodiak is the biggest bear.

Moose mothers carry their babies on their backs to cross the lake.

Do giraffes laugh? Let's find out!

Joke Time:
What always follows a hippopotamus?
Its tail!

What is the opposite of a gorilla?
A stop-rilla!

How are moose and ants different?
Moose have antlers, but ants don't have moose-lers!

What has antlers and eats cheese?
Mickey Moose!

What weighs four tons and wears glass slippers?
Cinder-elephant!

Where does an 8,000 pound rhino sleep?
Anywhere it wants to!

swallow

tree frog

inchworm

rabbit

mouse

bandicoot

ant   ladybug

elephant

giraffe

gorilla

moose

Kodiak

python

rhino

hippopotamus

STOP

37

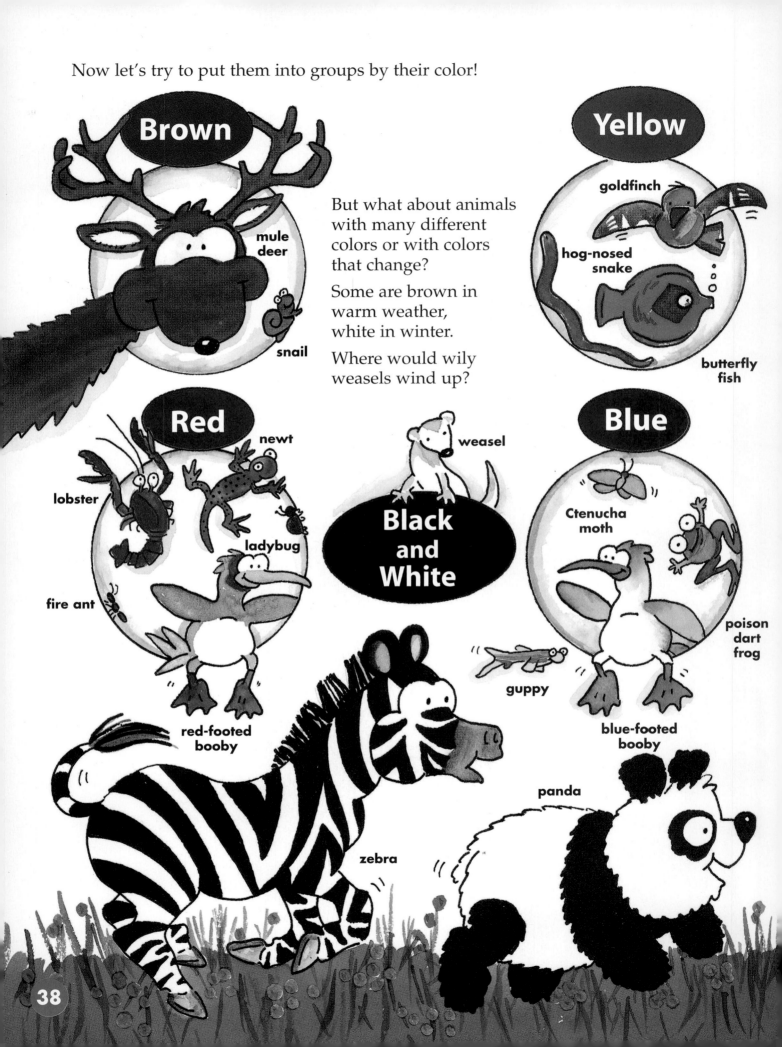

Now let's try to put them into groups by their color!

Brown

mule deer

snail

But what about animals with many different colors or with colors that change?

Some are brown in warm weather, white in winter.

Where would wily weasels wind up?

Yellow

goldfinch

hog-nosed snake

butterfly fish

Red

lobster

newt

ladybug

fire ant

red-footed booby

weasel

Black and White

Blue

Ctenucha moth

guppy

poison dart frog

blue-footed booby

panda

zebra

Or let's try to put them into groups by their ABC order!

Oh, no! Peter Peacock pecks Paul Puffin who passes puckery pickles to Patsy Pig as she paddles past in pink pajamas! Please, no! Paco Puma pounces in and pulls the plug! What a puddle of trouble!

Long ago a scientist named Sir Linneaus helped to fix this trouble. Starting when he was eight years old, Linneaus, a pastor's son, studied how all the animals grew and ate, where they lived, their habits, and how their bodies worked. Then he wrote down how to put some of them into the orderly groups we will study in the next chapters.

penguin

pepper moth

skunk

39

How many different groups of animals are there?

All the animals belong in two big groups: Animals with backbones
Animals without backbones

Feel the long bumpy bones going down your back. Most animals do not have backbones like you do. Have you ever felt a slimy slug or opened a shell at the beach and found a rubbery, blubbery clam? These are animals without backbones!

Animals without backbones usually do not have a face like you do either!

Snail eyes sit on the tips of their feelers! They can pop them in and out! Their silvery trail helps them to glide and slide along. God designed them so their shells spiral mostly to the right!

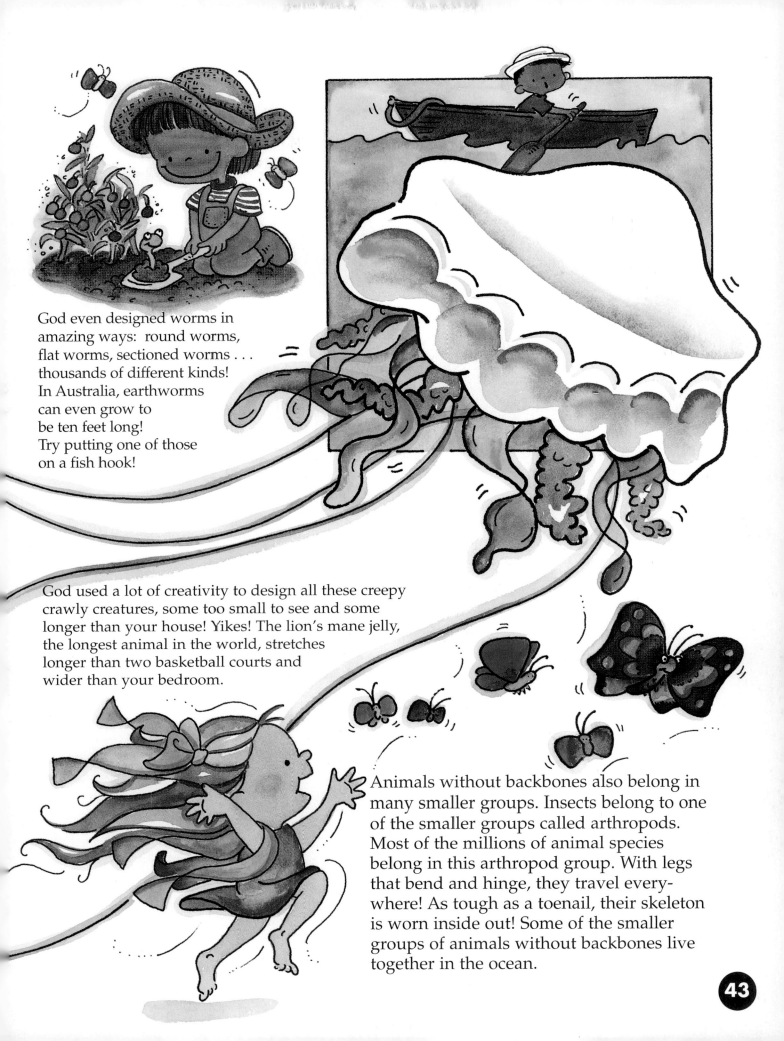

God even designed worms in amazing ways: round worms, flat worms, sectioned worms . . . thousands of different kinds! In Australia, earthworms can even grow to be ten feet long! Try putting one of those on a fish hook!

God used a lot of creativity to design all these creepy crawly creatures, some too small to see and some longer than your house! Yikes! The lion's mane jelly, the longest animal in the world, stretches longer than two basketball courts and wider than your bedroom.

Animals without backbones also belong in many smaller groups. Insects belong to one of the smaller groups called arthropods. Most of the millions of animal species belong in this arthropod group. With legs that bend and hinge, they travel every-where! As tough as a toenail, their skeleton is worn inside out! Some of the smaller groups of animals without backbones live together in the ocean.

Mollusks

Octopuses have eight arms. Squids have ten! Squids squirt to swim! "Is the octopus' birthday in October?" Who knows? God knows!

squid

octopus

The gooey duck stays in the same muddy underwater spot for over 100 years! Their long rubbery necks stretch out longer than a baseball bat!

oyster

clam

gooey duck

God designed over 2,000 different kinds of sea slugs!

sea slug

Arthropods

The snail shares its shell with a rascally hermit crab who shares it with a piggyback anemone!

No matter how small or odd, every animal God designed has an interesting story to tell.

shrimp

barnacles

soldier crab

Barnacles keep their legs hidden and stick to rocks with their secret glue.

Scientists still don't know how their glue stays stuck for thousands of years.

hermit crab

lobster

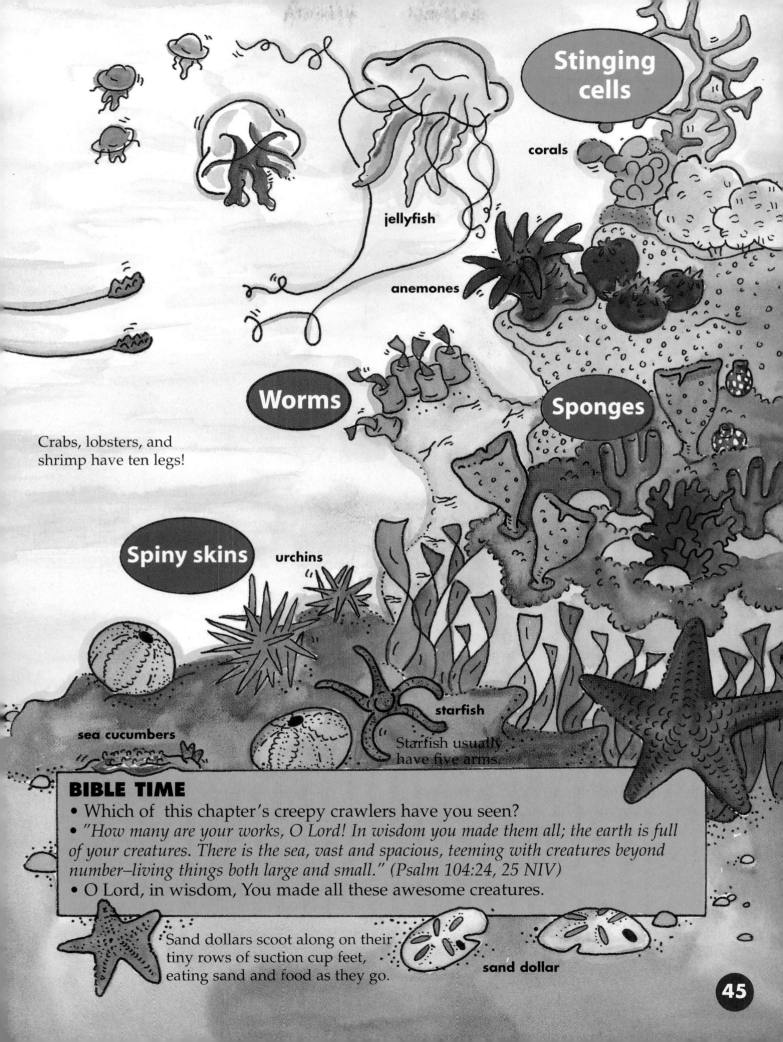

Stinging cells

corals

jellyfish

anemones

Worms

Sponges

Crabs, lobsters, and shrimp have ten legs!

Spiny skins

urchins

sea cucumbers

starfish

Starfish usually have five arms.

BIBLE TIME
- Which of this chapter's creepy crawlers have you seen?
- *"How many are your works, O Lord! In wisdom you made them all; the earth is full of your creatures. There is the sea, vast and spacious, teeming with creatures beyond number–living things both large and small."* (Psalm 104:24, 25 NIV)
- O Lord, in wisdom, You made all these awesome creatures.

Sand dollars scoot along on their tiny rows of suction cup feet, eating sand and food as they go.

sand dollar

Do bugs have noses?

grasshopper

stinkbug

Are all insects bugs? No! But all bugs are insects! Bugs are a smaller group of insects who are usually flat, with long feelers, and a sucker for a mouth.

Bugs do not have noses, but they do smell (especially stinkbugs)! Instead of noses, God designed insects with feelers called antennae. These feelers sense smell, touch, sound, and sometimes taste. Insects belong to the arthropod group and have bodies with three parts, six legs, and usually wings.

Here's another surprise: spiders, rolypolys, daddy long legs, centipedes, and scorpions are NOT bugs or insects! They have too many legs and no wings at all! But they are part of the arthropod group.

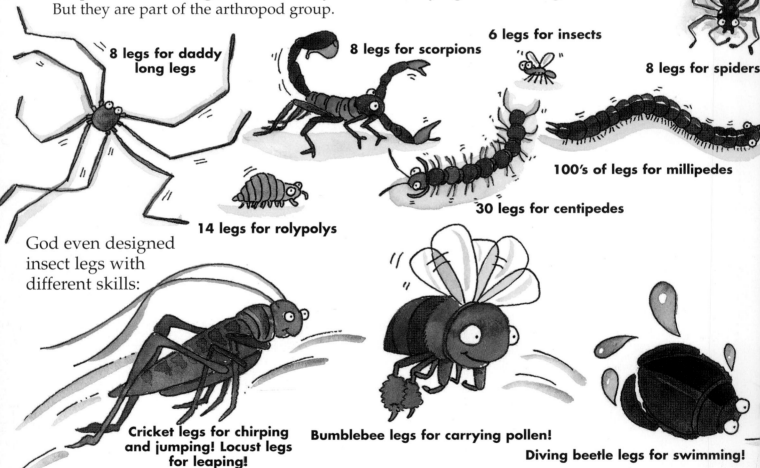

8 legs for daddy long legs

8 legs for scorpions

6 legs for insects

8 legs for spiders

14 legs for rolypolys

30 legs for centipedes

100's of legs for millipedes

God even designed insect legs with different skills:

Cricket legs for chirping and jumping! Locust legs for leaping!

Bumblebee legs for carrying pollen!

Diving beetle legs for swimming!

We often look at these little creepy crawlers as small and weak and unimportant, but God doesn't. He carefully designed each one with special skills. Sometimes, we look at ourselves as small and weak and unimportant, but God doesn't! He carefully designed each of us with special skills. He loves us! In the Bible, God says, *"I am with you; that is all you need. My power shows up best in weak people"* (2 Corinthians 12:9 TLB). Bugs, butterflies, and beetles are not big . . . but they are beautifully designed by God. Let's explore their unusual skills.

dragonfly

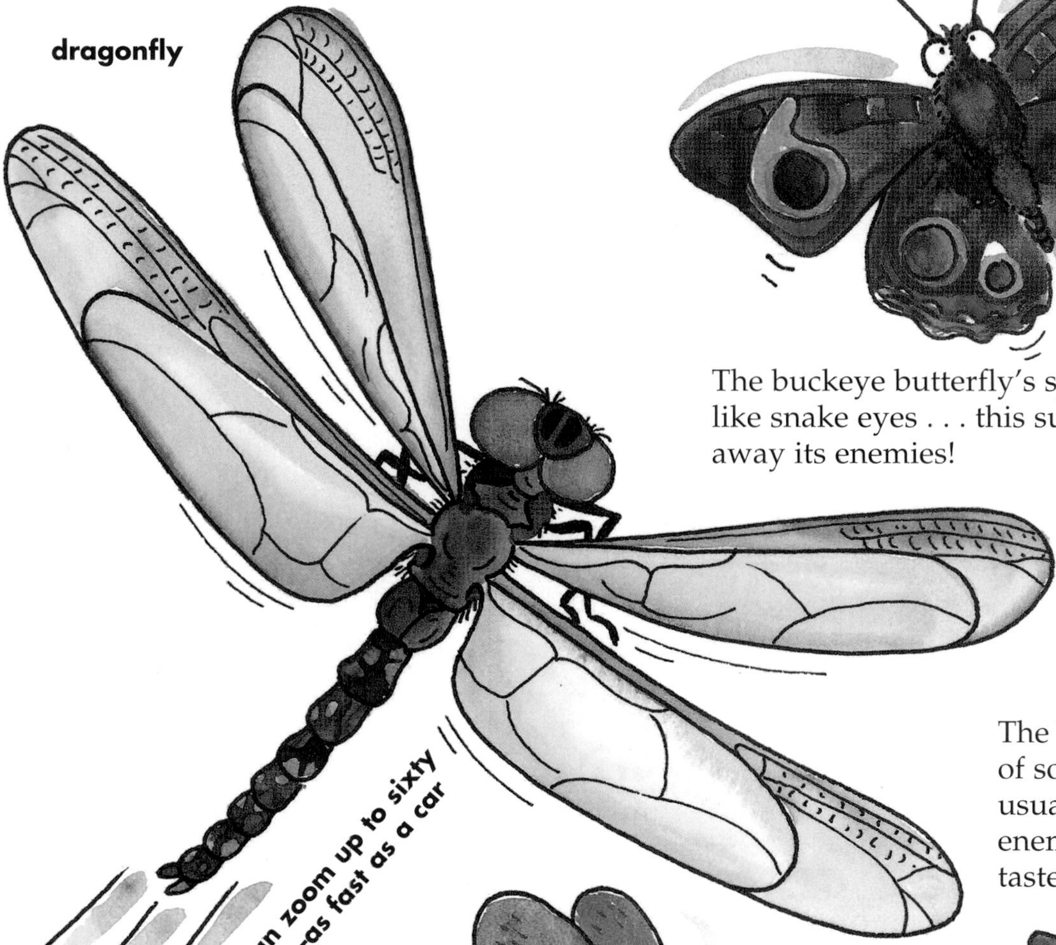

The buckeye butterfly's spots look like snake eyes . . . this sure scares away its enemies!

The bright colors of some insects usually tell their enemies that they taste yucky!

Dragonflies can zoom up to sixty miles per hour—as fast as a car on the freeway!

Fireflies shine their lights to find their friends in the dark!

Io moth

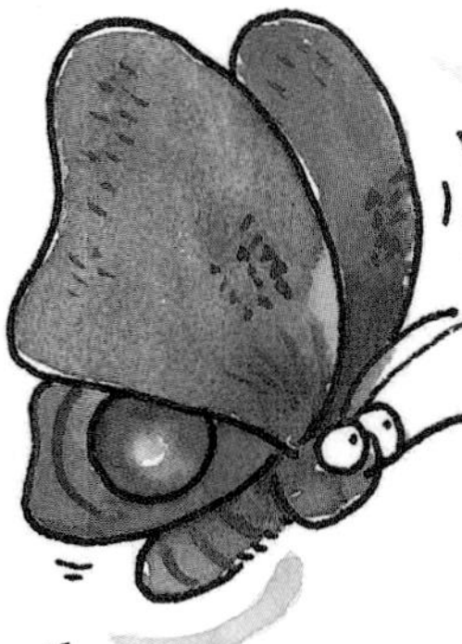

Do you like those party blowers? The tongues of moths and butterflies unroll to suck nectar out of flowers.

Even after bouncing around all day, the zebra butterfly remembers the very same leaf it slept on the night before. Butterflies look like flying flowers.

In which animal group can turtles be found?

Reptiles

Turtles belong to the group of animals WITH backbones. Animals WITH backbones also belong in five smaller groups.

Turtles belong to the reptile group. The granddaddy Galapagos turtle plods along for 150 years. He lives longer than any other animal or a person, but not longer than God! God always was, always is, and always will be! He is infinite. *"From everlasting to everlasting, you are God."* (Psalm 90:2 NIV) Can turtles climb out of their shells? No, because their backbones are stuck to the inside of their shells. They can't even change into pajamas at bedtime or brush their teeth. They don't have teeth! Turtles are the only reptiles with a shell and without teeth.

lizard

turtle

snake

tortoise

Amphibians

Joke Time: What do frogs dip in ketchup?

French flies!

Insects are the biggest GROUP of animals, but mammals are the group of the BIGGEST animals . . . even whales are mammals! Mammals are different from any other group because they have hair and make milk. Cows rule as our favorite milk-makers, but imagine yak yogurt, sheep shakes, mammoth milk and cookies! Yum!

Sea lions can "run" almost as fast as a person!

Although the tallest mammal, the giraffe has the same number of neckbones as the mouse, one of the smallest mammals!

God designed the armadillos to always have four matching babies!

The fennec fox is the tiniest fox, but her beautiful ears are the biggest!

Bears grow hair everywhere!

Mammals

Joke Time:
What's your cat's favorite breakfast food?
Mice Crispies!

giraffe

cat

mouse

bear

yak

sea lion

armadillos

52

BIBLE TIME
• Do mice belong to God? Do bears? Do cows? Do you?
• *"For every animal of the forest is mine, and the cattle on a thousand hills. I know every bird in the mountains, and the creatures of the field are mine." (Psalm 50:10, 11 NIV)*
• Thank You, God, that I belong to You, along with the mice and big bears!

How do cows make white milk out of green grass?
Who knows? God knows!

Bats, the only flying mammals,
help us by eating mosquitoes.

Mammoths are gone now,
but we still find their frozen fossils.

bat

cow

mammoth

sheep

fennec fox

53

How are salamanders and lizards different?

Amphibians begin their lives in water but their bodies change for life on land, too. Amphibians can breathe and drink through their skin–even underwater! Frogs and toads, newts and salamanders fill the amphibian group.

dart frog

chorus frog

Hi! I'm a salamander!
I am in the amphibian group.
Feel my soft, wet skin.

salamander

God knows about frog and toad toes. He designed amphibians differently from fish. Instead of fish fins, they have feet and toes. Tree frog toes have suction pads! Gliding frog toes have such large webs they can parachute down from branch to branch.

tree frog

toad

Cowabunga!

eggs

Toads often stay in the same neighborhood for thirty years.

toadlets

tadpoles

newt

When it's time to lay their eggs, newts often travel back to the pond where they were hatched.

What's green and jumps every three seconds?

A frog with hiccups!

Is croaking the sound of frogs joking? CROAK! CROAK!

Why did the little frogs paint themselves yellow, red, green, blue, brown and orange? So they could hide in the M&M's!

Are birds the only animals that fly?

Most birds fly, but so do most bugs and bats!
Most birds lay eggs in a nest, but so do turtles!
But only birds have feathers! Feathers make
birds different than any other animal.

Grenadier finch

Gouldian finch

bluebird

cardinal

starling

pigeon

Melba finch

mourning dove

Joke Time:
Which side of the chicken has the
most feathers? The outside!

58

meadowlark

fire finch

thrush

goldfinch

grosbeak

sparrow

warbler

cordonbleu finch

twinspot finch

cedar waxwing

scarlet tanager

phoebe

junco

God had lots of fun when He designed bird legs! Look at their feet. Which birds live in water?

crane

duck

penguin

golden eagle

wren

Ostriches cannot fly.
"Yet when she spreads her feathers to run, she laughs at horse and rider." (Job 39:18 NIV)
Ho, ho! Hee, hee!

The little jackrabbit is faster than both of them!

But the peregrine falcon is the fastest animal of all!

59

bluejay

grackle

baby robins

oriole

chickadee

woodpecker

Do you ever worry about going to a new class or your sick puppy? Are you scared of the dark? *"Don't worry . . . Look at the birds . . . your heavenly Father feeds them. And you know that you are worth much more than the birds."* (Matthew 6:25, 26 NCV)

Your worries are important to God. Because God is all-knowing and all-powerful, He is able to help us. Every time you see a bird flying through the sky, remember God is able to help you!

robin

nuthatch

kingfisher

How do hummingbirds hum? Their wings flap so fast they hum! Even though some hummingbirds weigh less than a dime, these tiniest of birds can fly non-stop over the sea for hundreds of miles!

Birds' eggs come in every color and size. A scientist who studies birds' eggs is called an oologist!

Owl eyes are so big they can't roll, so the owl rolls its head almost all the way around instead.

Puffins nest in underground tunnels!

puffin

ibis

owl

star finch

BIBLE TIME
• Do you have any worries? (A lost toy, night time, etc.)
• *"Not one sparrow . . . can fall to the ground without your Father knowing it."* (Matthew 10:29 TLB)
• Dear Lord, I'm glad You know my worries and that You are able to help me.

quail

Do only fish swim?

Look and see!

duck

Elephant trunks snorkel, shower, hug, lift, smell, and slurp.
Baby elephants even suck them like a thumb!

frog

elephant

Armadillos tip-toe
along the bottom or
float across the top.

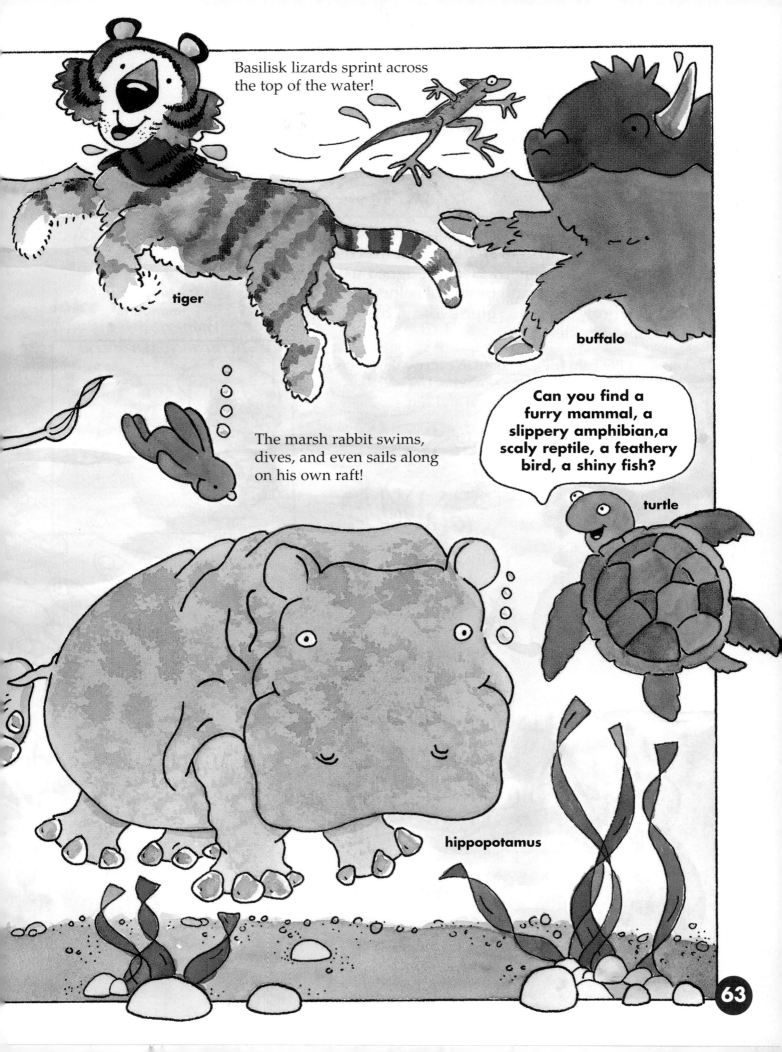

Basilisk lizards sprint across the top of the water!

tiger

buffalo

The marsh rabbit swims, dives, and even sails along on his own raft!

Can you find a furry mammal, a slippery amphibian, a scaly reptile, a feathery bird, a shiny fish?

turtle

hippopotamus

63

Which animals lived long ago?

Dinosaurs galore! Dinosaurs roar! Big ones stomping on boulders, little ones sitting on shoulders! Friendly ones, fighting ones! Plant-eaters, meat-eaters . . . YIKES! And God made them all! The warty, snorty dinosaurs remind us that we are not the bosses of the world! In power, a creature like the dinosaur *"ranks first among the works of God"* (*Job 40:19 NIV*).

A T-Rex's brain is smaller than his biggest tooth!
Iguanodon footprint fossils are found even in frozen Antarctica!
How do you like his spiky thumbs?

Tyrannosaurus Rex

Triceratops

Iguanodon

Saltopus

Diplodocus

JOKE TIME:

Why did the diplodocus paint her toenails red?
So she could hide in the strawberry patch!

What is yellow on the outside and green on the inside?
A school bus full of dinosaurs!

What has three horns and goes up-down, up-down?
A triceratops on a trampoline!

Parasaurolophus

Can caterpillars fly?

Can creepy, crawly caterpillars fly and glide high in the sky? Yes, after they change into butterflies! Only God could design them in this amazing way!

God designed each butterfly to begin as a tiny egg, then change into a caterpillar. Next it eats leaves, and more leaves, and even more leaves; while it sheds its first suit of skin, and another suit, and even another suit!

Finally, it hooks itself in a safe place, and sheds just once more. The last suit of skin hardens into the chrysalis case.

Somehow secretly inside, the caterpillar changes into jelly (not the kind you put on your sandwich!). No one knows how it does this, but God knows! And finally, it secretly changes from jelly into a butterfly!

satyr

skipper

cresent

zebra

Monarch caterpillar

Monarch chrysalis

Monarch butterfly

Guess who these babies change into:

Swallowtail butterfly and caterpillar

leafwing

hairstreak

Monarch

blue

Gloriously, it pops out of the chrysalis with wonderful, wind-catching, whispering wings!

Fly, fly! Bye, bye, butterfly!

ctenucha

"Yippee! It's me!"

child

jellyfish

penguin

God also designed frogs
and polliwogs to change in
an amazing way.
First, the eggs are laid.
Next, the eggs turn into
polliwogs. Then the legs
start to grow, while the
arms start to show,
and the tail
starts to go.

Finally, funny
frogs frolic,
finding flies
for food.
GUUUUULP!

Frogs change so they can live in water and on land. We must change so we can live in heaven. Because heaven—God's home—is a good and holy place. No sin, sadness, or badness can enter there. Sometimes we say, think, and do bad things. How could we ever live in heaven?

> *"Can a leopard change its spots?"*
> *(Jeremiah 13:23 NCV)* No!

Can we stop sinning all by ourselves? No!

Good news! God can change us! Because He is merciful and loving, He designed a way for us to change! *"When someone becomes a Christian he becomes a brand new person inside. He is not the same any more. A new life has begun!"* (2 Corinthians 5:17 TLB)

To become a Christian, you can say this prayer:
> *God, I have sinned and done bad things.*
> *I believe Jesus died on the cross for my sins.*
> *I believe He rose from the dead.*
> *Please forgive me and change me inside.*
> *Thank You for my new life!*

Because Jesus lives forever, we will too! When Jesus comes back to bring us home to heaven, He will even change our bodies into *". . . new bodies that will never, never die . . . but will live forever"* (1 Corinthians 15:52, 53 TLB). You will still be yourself, but your new body will never feel tired, sad, or sick.

BIBLE TIME
- Have you become a Christian yet?
- *"Listen, I tell you a mystery . . . we will all be changed–in a flash, in the twinkling of an eye, at the last trumpet. . . ."* (1 Corinthians 15:51, 52 NIV)
- Jesus, I want to thank You for my new body even before I wear it!

Will the animals ever be free again as in the Garden of Eden?

Because of sin–Adam and Eve's sin and our sin–the world is a mess. There are big problems, such as floods, hurricanes, earthquakes, sickness, and animal attacks. And there are smaller problems like mosquito bites and bee stings. All creation groans with frustration, waiting hopefully for its freedom from death and destruction, *"the glorious freedom of the children of God." (Romans 8:21 NIV)*

We're tired of hunting!   **We're tired of hiding!**

When Jesus comes back as **King of kings** and **Lord of lords**, He will fix everything by His mighty power! In the Bible, God tells us: *"Behold, I will create new heavens and a new earth . . . Be glad and rejoice forever in what I will create. . . ."* (Isaiah 65:17-18 NIV)

He will change:
Fear and fighting into fun and freedom.
Selfishness and survival into serving and helping.
Bungled jungles into places of oasis!

What will the animals do with all their skill and strength . . . just lie around in the sun? No way! There will be forests to explore, rivers to cross, maybe there will even be an Animal Olympics!

Gold Medal Jumpers

Big kangaroos jump the farthest.

But for their size, fleas are the champions, jumping 200 times the length of their body. If your daddy did this, he would jump the length of five city blocks!

Big 'ole elephants can't jump at all!

kangaroo

flea

Gold Medal Swimmers

Manta rays can burst out of the sea, soar through the sky, and have a baby manta ray in midair!

Penguins swim the fastest of the birds. The same size as a kindergartner, emperor penguins can dive deep down 800 feet, and hold their breath for almost twenty minutes!

manta ray

Leatherback turtles swim the fastest of the turtles, but green sea turtles, with their suits of shiny armor, swim the farthest.

green sea turtle

penguin

Gold Medal Weight Lifters

But elephants ARE weight lifters—the strongest of all!

But for their size, ants are even stronger, carrying stones fifty times their size with their jaws. If we did this, it would be like carrying an elephant with our teeth!

Gold Medal Gymnasts

Spotted skunks do handstands before they spray!

Gold Medal Runner

The cheetah!

dolphin

Dolphins swim the fastest of the mammals!

leatherneck turtle

As the big, blue sea is full of water, the new earth will be full of the Lord and His love. *"And may you be able to feel and understand, as all God's children should, how long, how wide, how deep, and how high his love really is… Now glory be to God who by his mighty power at work within us is able to do far more than we would ever dare to ask or even dream of. . . ."* (Ephesians 3:18-20 TLB)

Imagine the adventures! Maybe God will even bring back the extinct animals!

brachiosaurus

wolf

lion

calf

lamb

78

"In that day the wolf and the lamb will lie down together, and the leopard and goats will be at peace . . . a little child shall lead them all . . . The cows will graze among bears; Nothing will hurt or destroy in all my holy mountain, for as the waters fill the sea, so shall the earth be full of the knowledge of the Lord."
Isaiah 11:6-9 TLB

gibbon

lizard

goat

snail

guanaco

lemur

meerkats

leopard

bear

box turtle

BIBLE TIME:
- Which animal do you want to have an adventure with first?
- *"God richly gives us everything to enjoy." (1 Timothy 6:17 NCV)*
- God, we praise You for giving us the animals to enjoy and to teach us about You!

toad

goldfish

79

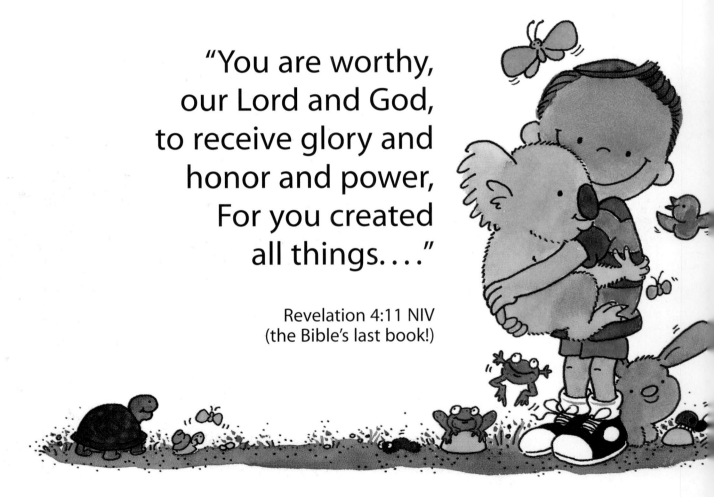

"You are worthy,
our Lord and God,
to receive glory and
honor and power,
For you created
all things...."

Revelation 4:11 NIV
(the Bible's last book!)

Faith Parenting Guide

Do Bugs Have Noses?

Age: 4-7 (Read-to-me)
8-12 (I-can-read-it-myself)

Life Issue: My child needs to understand that God created all things
and that God's creation shows us what He is like

Value: Creation/Faith

Learning Styles

Learning by seeing: We can see God's animal creation everywhere, as witnessed in picture books, on video, selected TV programs, or by visiting a zoo. Utilize these resources to show your child all the different animals that God created. Make a list of the animals you find. Talk about their differences. Emphasize that God created them all.

Learning by hearing: After reading this book, go to the library and find books that talk about animals. Start with those that are mentioned in this book and then expand your book choices to cover other animals. Read these books aloud to your child. Have fun making the sound that the animal makes and talk about the uniqueness of each animal God created.

Learning by touching: With clay, model animals that you and your child have seen. Talk to your child about God's creative power and the fun He must have had making all the animals. Talk about the big job Adam had in caring for the animals and naming each one. Let your child create an animal of his or her very own, and then name that animal.

*"And God said, 'Let the land produce living creatures according to their kinds.'
. . . And God saw that it was good." Genesis 1:24-25*